The Rise of the Empty People

Julia Golding ■ Dynamo

OXFORD
UNIVERSITY PRESS

TEAM X

Max, Cat, Ant and Tiger are four ordinary children with four extraordinary watches. When activated, their watches allow them to shrink to micro-size.

MAX — hologram communicator

CAT — magni-scope, tracking device

ANT — flip-up camera, video recorder

TIGER — warning light, torch

Previously ...

The watches were running low on power. Ant tried to recharge them using a machine that he had invented. However, during this process, something in the watches changed irrevocably.

When all the watches are synchronized, the micro-friends can travel through a rip in the fabric of space and time to other dimensions. Max, Cat, Ant and Tiger have become *rip-jumpers*.

Unfortunately, there is a problem. The rip has become permanently stuck open ... in Tiger's wardrobe! This leaves Earth – our Earth – open to attack.

A woman called **Perlest** came through the rip saying she wanted to help. She told the children that they needed to find the **Weaver**. Only he could seal the rip shut forever.

After many rip-jumps, the micro-friends found the Weaver, otherwise known as **Aracnan**. They took him back to their dimension. But it had all been a trick! The woman they knew as Perlest turned out to be her evil twin sister **Vilana**. She stole the Weaver's **Staff of Worlds**.

Now the children are trying to hunt down Vilana before she can use the Staff of Worlds to free her master, **Mordriss**, *The Dimension Reaper*.

Chapter 1 – Anyone home?

The city square was silent. Broken glass, fallen from high windows, glittered in the sunlight. Grey weeds grew undisturbed in the crevices between the stones. A jagged rip of blue light flashed: and then four pairs of feet thumped on the pavement, one after another.

Max rubbed the condensation from his watch, left over from what had just been a very cold rip-jump. He felt as though he had left his stomach somewhere between dimensions. 'Everyone OK?'

The other three signalled they were fine – if a little shaken.

Max checked the dimension number displayed on his watch. 'Zero, six, seven, two. Cat, is Vilana here?'

His friend adjusted the tracking settings on her watch. 'Yes – wait! No … Max, my watch is acting crazy. Something about this dimension is interfering with the signal.'

Ant had found something else to worry about. He knelt down and picked a leaf from one of the spiky weeds. It disintegrated into dust in his fingers.

'That's not good,' he said, puffing out his cheeks.

'What's wrong?' asked Tiger, crouching beside him.

'See this?' Ant plucked another leaf. That one also crumbled. 'The plants have been fried.'

'You mean they're burnt?' asked Cat.

'Yes, and not by the sun.' Ant looked up at the sky and corrected himself: '*Suns*. They appear to have two in this dimension.'

Cat curled her lip in distaste. 'I wouldn't mind living in a twin-sun dimension with sandy beaches and palm trees, but this one is just creepy. Where is everyone?'

Max turned slowly, taking in the skyscrapers that surrounded the city square. Most of them had gaping holes where there had once been glass. The surfaces of the remaining doors were blackened or bubbled in paint-blisters. A sky-rail looped between the buildings, but there were no trains running on the tracks.

'Cat's right. We're in the middle of a large city but there's nobody about, even though it's broad daylight,' he said. 'That's just not right.'

Cat scuffed the broken glass with the toe of her boot. 'Perhaps there was a war and the city was abandoned?'

'Or maybe something even worse has happened?' suggested Ant. 'I can't hear anything – not even birds.'

Cat shuddered. Her instincts were telling her not to loiter here in the open. They had a mission; the disaster that had befallen this place wasn't their business. 'Look, guys, let's get going. I don't want to stay here any longer than we have to. If Vilana is hiding in this dimension, we need to track her down.'

Tiger brushed the dust off his knees. 'Relax, Cat. If there's no one here, we've got nothing to worry about. We've got a whole city to explore!'

Ant nodded, tilting his face up to enjoy the sunshine. 'Ah, it feels so good to be warm again. I wouldn't mind a closer look at that sky-rail. I wonder how it's powered. Probably solar energy, in a world with two suns.'

Max kicked a blackened piece of wood away from a fallen statue of a woman. She was clad in armour and had once been riding a bronze horse. Now that she and her mount were on their side, the four hooves and two feet were pointing out obliquely.

'Maybe we'll be able to spare a few minutes to look around, but don't forget our priority is finding Vilana,' Max said. 'We need to get the Staff of Worlds back. Let's get going … We might pick up Vilana's trail if we keep moving.'

'I hope so. We don't have time for sightseeing.'

so much depends on us,' Cat replied, looking pointedly at Ant and Tiger.

Max led the way towards the nearest road leading out from the square. The friends had to weave between burnt-out vehicles and more fallen statues.

'Looks like they had some kind of magnetic road surface for the cars,' observed Ant, pointing at the twisted metal gleaming in the potholed surface. 'I wish we could have seen it before it was ruined.'

'It's what caused all this devastation that's worrying me,' murmured Cat.

With a sudden movement, Tiger gripped her elbow. Cat almost jumped out of her skin.

'Cut it out!' Cat snapped – she was unnerved enough without him playing stupid jokes on her.

'I'm not joking! Wait! Stop, guys!' Tiger called urgently to Max and Ant.

The boys turned round.

'What's up?' asked Max.

'I saw someone.' Tiger gestured towards the dark entrance to an underground station twenty metres away. 'Just a glimpse, but there was definitely movement.'

'What do we do?' asked Ant. 'Make a run for it?'

Max shook his head. 'We don't know what we

would be running towards – maybe more danger. I'd prefer to find out who's down there.'

'It's a bad idea,' said Cat, shaking her head.

Max walked towards the entrance of the station. 'Hello? Anyone there?'

Cat's instincts screamed a warning. She agreed with Ant: they should make a dash for it out of the square. 'Please, Max, get away from there!'

Max ignored her protests and called, 'You, down there: it's OK. We won't hurt you.' He looked back at his friends and shrugged. 'Nothing. Are you sure you saw someone, Tiger?'

'Positive.' Tiger's expression was grim. He was definitely not playing a joke on them.

'Watch out, Max!' Cat moved closer to Tiger as she spotted movement around them. 'Tiger's right – and there's more than one of them.'

The pale figure of a woman appeared in one window on the first floor of a nearby building. She stood observing them blankly, swaying slightly. Then a man emerged from the darkness of the station, standing at the top of the stairs.

Max took a wary step away. The friends drew closer together, standing back to back so they could watch every corner of the square. One by one, people began to fill the doorways of the square. They were tall and thin, like shadows seen in the late afternoon: long, stretched limbs, thin necks, narrow heads. Their eyes stared ahead, unfocused. They were dressed in the remnants of what had once been fine clothes. Slowly, they moved in on the friends.

'I really don't like this. What's wrong with them?' whispered Ant.

'They're moving like sleepwalkers,' muttered Tiger.

'Asleep or awake, there are too many of them,' said Max.

'Shall we rip-jump out of here?' asked Ant.

'And lose Vilana? No way,' Tiger said fiercely. 'That's just what she'd want us to do. She's obviously led us to this dimension to try to stop us. We should make a break for one of the roads leading out of this square. These people are so slow, we can easily outrun them.'

The walker nearest to Cat swiped at her with his arm in a clumsy motion. She ducked and backed away. He lunged again – and missed.

'Quickly: I can't keep dodging him forever!' cried Cat urgently. The walkers seemed to be trying to split up the friends. 'Whatever we decide, I vote we do it right now!' She tried to circle around to rejoin her friends. 'I'm pretty sure they're *not* harmless.'

But it was too late! A manhole cover right by Cat's feet clanged open; a hand snaked out and grabbed her ankle. With a panicked yelp, she tried to free her foot but the grip was too strong – something was pulling her down into the hole. 'Help!'

'Cat!' shouted Max. He rushed towards her but another walker rose from inside one of the burnt-out cars and caught the back of his top in claw-like hands. A second lurched out of the shadows and grabbed Max's wrist, preventing him from reaching his watch.

A further three walkers had Ant cornered against one of the fallen statues. Tiger was struggling to dodge around the walkers between him and Cat, but they kept him back with swipes of their lanky arms.

'Guys! Do something!' Cat was slipping down into the darkness, with only her head and shoulders still above ground. She thought about reaching for her watch but she knew she couldn't risk losing her grip on the pavement.

In desperation, Tiger dived between the legs of the nearest walker. His fingertips touched Cat's just as her grip finally loosened and she vanished down the hole.

'No!' he shouted. But Cat was gone.

Chapter 2 – **Survivors**

'Cat!' Tiger dangled his head over the hole, straining to see his friend in the dark, dank space below.

'Get back!' warned Max. 'We can't lose you as well. We've got to stick together … We can save her as long as we're together.'

Tiger moved away just in time: a blast of flame suddenly erupted from the hole. Showing the first sign of fear, the walkers surrounding the boys instantly shuffled back, leaving a ring of about ten metres clear around them. More flames rippled through the air on the far side of the square.

Ant jumped up on to the plinth of the statue to get a better look. 'I think help has arrived! I can see more people – and they've got flame-throwers. The walkers seem to be scared of the heat or the light, or both.'

As the boys watched anxiously, the walkers retreated into the buildings and underground station like insects seeking a rock under which to hide. As soon as the way was clear, Max, Ant and Tiger hurried back to the manhole.

'We need to go after Cat!' said Tiger. He called down into the hole. 'Cat? Are you there? We're coming for you.'

'No, stay there.' Cat's voice sounded very distant. 'Get away from the manhole and wait.'

Tiger moved to stand with Max and Ant. All around them, small groups of people emerged from the streets leading into the square. They were equipped with flame-throwers and were using them to herd the walkers away. They weren't aiming directly at the walkers; they seemed to be using the bursts of fire to scare them off.

'They look the same as the walkers …' said Ant thoughtfully.

'But they move normally whereas the walkers look like they are only half-awake,' finished Max.

Finally, all the strange walkers had been herded away from the square. The boys heard a scraping sound in the manhole and Cat's head and shoulders emerged, boosted up by someone below. Max and Tiger pulled her the rest of the way up.

'Oh, am I glad to see you!' she said, smiling with relief. 'Here, help the others up.'

'Others?' asked Tiger.

'Yeah, they've been clearing the drains of walkers.'

Reaching back into the hole, Max and Tiger gave a hand to three people: two men and a girl. As they emerged, it was clear they were all wearing a kind of uniform – a grey camouflage, clearly designed to mingle in with the urban landscape around them. The girl had her blonde hair tied neatly in a plait. The men had short brown hair and tired-looking faces. The men and the girl each had a flame-thrower in their hands, the tank strapped to their back. They were really tall, far taller than any adult from the friends' own dimension.

There was an awkward silence as they all waited

for someone to be the first to speak.

'We ... um ... don't mean anyone any harm,' said Max, wishing he had a better line to offer.

The girl smiled wryly, her blue eyes twinkling. The expression made her seem a hundred times more approachable than the formidable warrior girl who had emerged from the manhole. 'That's good to hear. We've got enough problems here without more hostiles arriving. Who are you and where are you from? Don't you know how stupid it is to walk about the city without one of these?' She tapped her flame-thrower.

We do now, Max was thinking as he held out a hand. 'I'm Max. This is Ant and Tiger. Cat, you've already met. We … er … came from another country and have only just arrived. We had no idea that we were in danger.'

The girl arched a brow at his hand, not sure how to respond. She then held her hand out in the same way, making no attempt to touch his. She clearly thought this was the polite way of greeting strangers where they came from. 'You didn't know? You didn't know about *them*?'

'Them?' asked Tiger.

'The Empty People. Doesn't your country have them?' She gestured to the doorways into which the walkers had disappeared.

'I don't think so,' said Max, letting his hand fall to his side.

The girl's face lit up with hope. 'That's wonderful news. You'd better come back with us and tell us all about it. Joel, Merrie, can we take them back to the hideout?'

The two men who had been standing guard exchanged a glance. One of them had a beard; he stroked it thoughtfully and said, 'There's been no mist since you arrived?'

Max shook his head, wondering why he had asked such an odd question. 'No. It's been like this – sunny and clear.'

'All right, Goldie, we can take them back with us,' the bearded man said to the girl. 'They can't stay here in any case. It isn't safe.'

'Thanks, Merrie. Come on, we have to hurry. The flame-throwers only send the Empty People into hiding for a short time; they come back when our canisters run out.' Goldie touched Max's elbow, guiding him away.

'What happens then?' asked Max.

Goldie shuddered. 'You don't want to know. Let's just say that it's better for everyone if we are in the hideout before that happens.'

Max, Cat, Ant and Tiger followed their new friend through the deserted streets of the city, the two men watching their back. Goldie's nervousness was contagious. Everywhere the friends looked, they could see the same devastation. Normal life had stopped in its tracks.

'What happened here?' asked Ant, running to catch up with Goldie. 'I mean with the Empty People.'

She looked surprised to be asked. 'I thought everyone knew.'

'We don't,' asserted Max. 'Please tell us.'

Goldie led them to the entrance of the tallest skyscraper they had seen yet. It reached up to the skies above them: a thin needle of a building with more windows intact than the surrounding towers. 'I hope you're all fit – we've got quite a climb ahead. It's one of the many ways we deter the Empty People from following us.'

'Anything to get away from them,' said Cat, voicing everyone's thoughts.

They began climbing the stairs. Goldie explained that the lifts were out of action, along with all the other machines in the city.

'The Empty People appeared with the mist,' said Goldie, picking up the story now they were on the way to safety. 'You can't imagine how lovely it was here before. It was a wonderful place to live – crowds of people, lots of things to do, parks and gardens to enjoy. Then one day, a purple mist spread out from the presidential palace and our leader disappeared. He hasn't been seen since – nor have any of his guards or government ministers.'

'What happened to the mist?' asked Ant.

Goldie shrugged. 'It cleared, and we thought that was it – we were too busy trying to find the missing people. But the palace was locked up tight and no one could get in. Crowds waited outside, hoping to glimpse President Falen, but instead the mist appeared again. When it dispersed, the whole crowd at the gates had been turned into them … the Empty People.' Her eyes were shining with tears. 'No one is immune. Entire families fell under the curse of the mist that day. We learned to hide when the mist appeared, but still each week some of us get caught outside. It's a terrible dilemma. We can't stay up here all the time because we have to find food, but we take a horrible risk going down to the ground. Only up here, above the level of the mist, is it safe.'

'How do you think the mist works?' Ant asked with a frown.

'We don't know. My uncle Joel thinks the mist is some kind of accelerated bio-chemical reactant that changes our DNA, but we can't get a sample without falling under its power ourselves.'

Cat pondered the implications of Goldie's words as she climbed the stairs. A painful stitch had begun to build in her side. It seemed an endless climb, with Goldie constantly unbolting and rebolting a series of heavy metal doors. On the last level, Goldie knocked on the door and a guard inside opened it. The four friends followed Goldie in and found themselves in a space filled with scores of sleeping mats, bundles of clothes and food, and suitcases. The large windows gave a stunning view of a double sunset over the distant mountains – they were clearly on the observation deck.

'Welcome to the hideout,' said Goldie. 'One of the only safe places in the city of Trist.'

Chapter 3 – **Purple mist**

That night, after a late meal cooked over an open fire on the windy narrow rooftop of the skyscraper, the friends looked out over the dark city. Apart from the glow of a handful of other fires on the tops of neighbouring skyscrapers, there was only one light visible across the entire roofscape. It shone in the darkness like a bright white eye keeping a sinister watch over the silent metropolis.

'What's that?' Cat asked Goldie, indicating the strange building.

'It's the presidential palace,' Goldie explained. 'It's the only building lit up because it's the only building with any power.

No one knows how it's powered but …' She paused, almost unwilling to continue.

'But what?' Ant gently nudged.

'Well, that's where the Empty People live. I mean, it's their main base. That's where they take you if you're caught. They force you into the mist cloud so you become one of them.'

The friends peered down into the dark. There was no sign of any Empty People. Like bees in a hive, they all seemed to have quieted down for the night.

Shivering, the friends went inside and settled down in a corner of the hideout near Goldie, Joel and Merrie. Joel and Merrie were her uncles, Goldie had explained over supper. Her parents and little sister had been caught in the mist three months ago, but she had not given up hope of finding them. Surely, too, there would eventually be a way of curing the disease.

'I can't abandon hope,' she told Max and the others, showing them a picture of her family before the mist had descended on them. Four happy faces smiled up at them, but now only Goldie remained. 'We have to beat this or there will be none of us left.'

* * * * * *

'It's awful for her,' whispered Ant, when he thought their new friend was asleep. 'I don't know how she dares go down to the ground, knowing what happened to her family.'

'It's as she says: they have no choice. They have to eat,' said Max.

'What will they do when there is nothing in the city

left to scavenge?' Cat asked.

No one had an answer. The people of this dimension were in a dire situation, but what could be done to help them?

'If only someone could find out what it is in the mist that turns them into Empty People. If they knew that, maybe they could find the antidote?' suggested Ant.

'Well, I'd start with the presidential palace. That's where we're going to find answers,' said Tiger decisively.

'It's not safe!' Max exclaimed. 'After everything Goldie's told us, you really want to lead us straight into the heart of the Empty People?'

'There's got to be someone else there,' said Cat, rubbing her arms to get warm. 'I don't think it's just the Empty People. They're more like empty shells than living people – how could they possibly create power?'

'Well, they certainly give me the creeps,' grumbled Ant. 'And I'm not the one who was pulled into that hole by them.' He hesitated. 'How long do you think we should stay here, Max? We could, you know, just rip-jump out of here.' Ant looked a little ashamed to make the suggestion.

'We can't!' Cat was almost shouting. She looked round to check Goldie hadn't stirred. 'We can't leave Goldie. And besides,' Cat showed him her watch, 'Vilana is cropping up again on my readout. And guess what? The signal looks like it's coming from …'

'The presidential palace,' finished Tiger.

'This situation could well be a key part of our mission – not separate from it,' argued Cat.

Max nodded. 'Yes, this is just the kind of horrible mess Vilana would enjoy. If she's not behind it, I wouldn't be surprised to find her at least taking advantage of it. We can't forget we have our own mission to complete and, to do that, we need to know for sure whether Vilana is here.'

'So I suppose we have to try to get into the palace,' said Ant bravely.

'I'm afraid so. But not tonight. Let's sleep and see what the morning brings,' replied Max.

Tiger nodded and curled up under a blanket. 'Good plan.'

* * * * * *

The morning was overcast, with a chill in the air. Goldie seemed surprised when the friends volunteered to come on her trip to find supplies.

'This isn't your battle,' she said, strapping on her flame-thrower. 'You should make arrangements to get out of here. That story you gave last night at supper about being lost and ending up here doesn't make much sense, you know. The Council of Elders wants to question you later, check the facts and find out if your country might take us as refugees.'

The friends exchanged concerned looks. If the people here discovered that they could rip-jump to another dimension, wouldn't they all demand to leave with them? They had to keep their watches a secret or they would never get the chance to catch up with Vilana and rescue the Staff of Worlds.

'Council of Elders?' asked Max.

'Yes,' said Goldie. 'The elders are the people who took over when the president disappeared. They're the ones who organize our hiding places and set out the rules – like how we must all share the provisions we find. There's a representative in each of the skyscrapers that are used as hideouts. This is the biggest and most important hideout so the head of the council stays here. She's over there.' Goldie pointed to a weary-looking white-haired woman dressed in green, who was sitting on a box on the rooftop listening to a circle of people who all seemed to be talking at once. 'That's Ida's morning court,' Goldie explained. 'You can bring your problems to her and she'll try to find a solution. She won't have time to talk to you until after noon, but I know she's keen to find out more about where you came from.'

'That's fine, we can come back then. For the moment, we want to help you look for food,' said Max.

They soon discovered that it was no easier going down the many flights of stairs than it had been coming up. After a while it was hard not to stumble, the treads blurring before their eyes.

'Hold on to the banister,' advised Goldie. 'And try not to think too hard about your feet.'

Out on the street, Goldie scanned the buildings with a pair of binoculars, checking for threats. She was very impressive in the way she scoped out the terrain, making the friends feel confident that she would do her best to keep them safe.

'Joel and Merrie are doing a long trip to the abandoned markets on the edge of the city today, so I need to stay close to the base,' she explained.

'Can you take us closer to the presidential palace?' asked Tiger. 'We'd like to have a look after we saw the lights last night.'

'I don't blame you: we're all intrigued by the lights. They shine every evening and no one knows how. The building must have its own power source, but we don't know what kind or who is responsible for it.' Goldie started walking in the direction of the palace. 'I can take you a little closer, but it is too risky to get within sight of the walls. There are too many Empty People inside and the fence itself is dangerous.'

'How dangerous? Is it electrified?' asked Tiger.

Goldie shook her head. 'We don't think so. It's defended, but we aren't sure how, as no one who has managed to get in has returned to tell the tale. I've promised my uncles that I won't go too close, but the streets around the palace are a good place to scavenge so I can take you in that direction.'

Goldie led them to a vast shop with windows that looked out on the palace grounds. It was eerie standing in a deserted showroom with clothes still on the mannequins, shiny shoes on the racks, and trays of jewellery there for the taking. Goldie explained that because you couldn't eat gems or precious metals, they were now without value. She was far more interested to see if there were any remaining stocks of cakes and biscuits in the food hall. The friends followed her in, looking around. The room was unrecognizable as a food hall – every single shelf had been ransacked of all its goods. Goldie carried on into the small stockroom and eventually re-emerged clutching just one, fairly crushed, packet of biscuits.

Tiger stood gazing out at the mysterious palace. A white building with columns at the front supporting a gabled roof – it looked very grand and solemn. Unlike the rest of the city, the building and its gardens appeared to be carefully maintained.

'Hey, I can see gardeners at work!' he called.

'That's right, but they're all Empty People,' replied Goldie, not looking round. 'We don't know why they carry on working. Anytime we try to talk to one we capture, we're met with a complete blank. They've no idea why they do anything.'

Max, Cat and Ant joined Tiger at the window.

'I can't see them,' said Ant. 'There seems to be some kind of haze in the way.'

'Haze? As in mist?' Goldie rushed to their side. 'Oh no – we've got to run!' The vapour was rapidly rising from the ground, thickening until they could see its purple hue. 'There's no time to get back to the hideout. We have to climb to the top floor … now!' She dropped her bag and raced for the emergency stairs to the roof. The friends caught her urgency and sprinted after her. But the stairwell door was locked. There was no choice – they'd have to climb as high as they could within the shop building. They dashed up the internal stairs to the top floor, but the building was only five storeys tall. Would it be enough?

Goldie led them into the department that had once sold furniture. With their help, she quickly piled up the tables and chairs so they could ascend even higher – almost to the ceiling. 'This is as high as we can get. If the mist arrives, try not to breathe it in,' she instructed, panting.

In agonizing silence, the friends waited with Goldie, attempting to guess how long it would take the cloud of mist to envelop them. The mist was even worse than the Empty People; at least with the people, flame-throwers could be used to scare them off. But nothing could stop the mist.

Before long, a pale purple cloud curled through a broken window like a snake. It was followed by more tendrils, winding across the display room, creeping over chairs and tables.

Covering her mouth and nose with her palm, Goldie sobbed. 'I'm sorry. I should never have brought you here.' She held out her hand, offering the gesture Max had taught her. With eyes full of sympathy, Cat took Goldie's hand in hers.

'We could always rip-jump,' whispered Ant.

'But we can't take her with us,' hissed Tiger.

'I'm so sorry, Goldie. We have no choice.' Max lifted his wrist. 'Ant, set the dials for *any* dimension now.'

'But we haven't found Vilana …' Cat protested.

'We just need to go!' Max cried.

But they had not acted swiftly enough. A tongue of mist wound up Max's body and filled his nose with a faint flowery odour. Goldie keeled over, tumbling off her tower of furniture to the floor and was immediately completely covered by a purple blanket of vapour. The friends watched in horror as the tendrils of mist began to crawl into her nose, mouth and ears … It even covered her eyes.

'Stop!' cried Ant, as Max was about to turn his dial. 'If this disease is catching, we can't risk taking it to another dimension – or letting any mist through the rip.'

He was right and they all knew it.

'I'm sorry, guys,' said Max, dropping his wrist. 'You are the best team ever. I'm proud to have known you.'

Grimly, they all lowered their wrists and waited for the mist to envelop them.

Chapter 4 – **No safe place**

Cat rubbed her eyes. They had been sitting in the mist for ten full minutes, but now it was dissipating and she could see her friends again. They clung to their high perches on the furniture, eyes bleak with despair, as the fog finally rolled away.

'Is everyone OK?' Cat asked softly. She could finally make out Goldie lying on the floor. She wasn't moving.

Tiger clambered down to Goldie's side. 'She's still breathing. Wake up, Goldie! Wake up!'

Her blue eyes opened, but there was no life in them. She opened her mouth and groaned, no proper words forming.

'Get back, Tiger!' warned Ant. 'She's one of them now!'

Tiger refused to move. 'But she's our friend!'

Goldie staggered to her feet, swaying precariously, limbs moving as if attached to weights. It was horrible to watch.

Max jumped down. 'She doesn't look dangerous.

Let's take her back to her uncles and see if they can help her. Maybe she didn't get a full dose of the mist?'

Cat shook her head. 'I don't think that's likely. We've been covered in it for a long time. All of us have been breathing it in.'

'So why aren't we like her?' asked Ant.

'I don't know.' Max frowned. 'Maybe … maybe being from a different dimension gives us some kind of immunity?'

'I'd prefer not to stand around talking about this. Let's head back before the mist – or some Empty People – find us,' suggested Cat. 'I'll take Goldie's flame-thrower. She can't use it now.'

The friends guided the stumbling Goldie down the stairs and back along the street to the hideout. When they reached the entrance to the skyscraper, they were relieved to see Joel and Merrie approaching from the opposite direction, both shouldering huge bags of supplies.

'Hey, over here!' called Max.

Joel and Merrie dropped their bags and sprinted towards them.

'What are you doing?' shouted Joel. His face was milk-white with shock as he saw Goldie lurching from side to side.

'We got caught in that mist and Goldie's … well, you can see for yourself,' explained Ant. 'We were hoping you could help her.'

Joel let out a heartbreaking howl of anguish. 'Not Goldie!'

Merrie fell to his knees, fists clenched.

'Look, she's not dangerous,' said Cat, leading Goldie round by the hand. 'She doesn't seem to know what's happening.'

'You don't understand: once she meets another Empty Person, then she'll join their collective mind. They have only one mind – one will – driving them,' said Merrie, with a terrible sadness in his voice. He got to his feet and cupped his niece's cheek tenderly. 'She'll try to herd you to the palace. Why did it have to be you? Goodbye, Goldie.'

'But you can't just let her go!' spluttered Tiger in outrage. 'Why not keep her on her own, away from the others?'

'And then what?' asked Joel bitterly. 'She would be walking around in circles in a room all day. I cannot put my own niece in such a prison, even if I think it is safer for her. At least with the others she has some kind of life – a half-life but one where she is able to move freely.' He looked down; the hunch of his shoulders told the friends that this quarantine had been tried for others before – and had failed.

'So we just let her go?' asked Cat, aghast.

'Yes. The Council of Elders has forbidden any of us to bring Empty People into the hideout. Don't you think we'd all help our loved ones if we had a choice? But the law was made to protect both us and them. Once in the mist, they have to go and join others like them.' Joel kissed the top of Goldie's head. 'Go on, sweetheart.'

The friends were speechless as Goldie shuffled back the way they had come. As she reached the end of the street, another Empty Person stepped out of a station entrance and touched her shoulder. Goldie turned as if she was in a dream and disappeared down the stairs to the subterranean tunnels.

'This is crazy!' Tiger was furious. 'I can't believe you just booted her out like that!'

Joel's eyes glittered with rage and sorrow. 'You have no right to an opinion about this. Until you've lived here as long as we have and made the hard choices we've had to make … what do you know about anything anyway?'

Merrie squeezed Joel's arm to placate him. 'Brother, we are missing something important: why are these children not Empty People by now?'

Only something so startling could distract Joel from his grief. He took a step away from them, examining them for warning signs. 'You're right, Merrie. I've never known anyone go through the mist and come out the same.'

Merrie gestured to Ant, the smallest of the group. 'We've already remarked that the people from their country are particularly short and round. Maybe they also have a natural protection against the disease?'

Joel beckoned them to follow. 'Come on. There is much we have to tell the Council of Elders and many questions they will want answering.'

Chapter 5 – Tiger in trouble

The elder known as Ida studied the friends carefully. 'You've breathed in the mist but it did nothing to you?' she asked. She was softly spoken, but there was a steely will behind the question. Max knew that Ida would not hesitate to expel them from the hideout if she thought they were a threat.

'That's right. We smelt it – could even taste it on our tongues – but nothing changed. Only Goldie was affected,' Max answered honestly.

The ring of council members muttered among themselves at this startling news. The friends had the feeling that, even though they were clearly not Empty People, there were few in the room who would be so keen to welcome them now.

'I would like our doctors to look at you,' announced Ida. 'It would be very useful if we could isolate what makes you immune. Perhaps you are the clue we require to find a cure?' Ida's grey eyes watched for their reaction.

'We … er … I suppose that's OK,' said Max, glancing round at the others for their opinion. Really, he didn't think it was OK at all. They would have to find a way to avoid being examined: he wasn't sure what the medics would find if they ran tests. At the moment, the locals hadn't raised the possibility that the friends were from another dimension altogether, and Max preferred to keep it that way.

'Of course you can check us over,' said Cat. 'We'll do anything to help Goldie.' She gave the others a hard look.

'Good. Then I'll send a message to the hospital tower and ask one of the doctors to come over and examine you. Until then, don't go anywhere.' Ida folded her hands in her lap, waiting for their reply. Each question and answer was like a move in a game of chess against a very skilled player.

'But aren't you going to do something to save Goldie?' exploded Tiger, having had enough of this ponderous discussion. 'I can't believe I just saw her packed off to those Empty People! Aren't you going to do anything?'

Ida looked away, pained by the weight of her responsibility. 'She has become one of them, young man. I don't expect you to understand. It has taken us all a long time to adjust to the idea that there is nothing we can do to save one of our own once the mist takes hold.'

'We'll see about that,' Tiger muttered.

The four friends moved away from Ida. Two guards took up position at the door, clearly posted there to stop them leaving.

Max looked torn, as if he was searching for an answer. He put his hand to his head. 'We haven't got time for them to examine us. We need to leave.'

'We can't do that!' protested Cat. 'I meant what I said about wanting to help Goldie. If we are immune to the mist, we'd be doing this whole dimension a massive favour by letting their doctors study us.'

'That's a huge risk,' said Ant, looking nervously around – but no one was close enough to eavesdrop. 'They might work out that we're not from this dimension.'

'Then we'll just have to make up a very good story.' Cat paced restlessly. 'Come on, guys: rip-jumping away from this trouble feels like exactly the kind of thing Vilana would do. And, anyway, we *still* need to confirm whether she's in this dimension.'

That settled it. They looked for a place to rest and make plans, but no one wanted them in their family groups, hurrying to pick up small children if they stumbled into their path. The taint of the mist lingered about them. Max led them back to sit in the circle of Goldie's old belongings. Cat sniffed and wiped her eyes on the cuff of her sleeve as she looked at the hairbrush Goldie had used that morning to part her hair.

'This is just awful,' said Ant sadly. 'Cat and Tiger are right: we've got to do something for Goldie.'

'I know. But what?' Max asked.

'It will take more investigation and careful planning. We need to try to get back to the palace. Don't you think so, Tiger?' Ant looked round, but Tiger was nowhere to be seen. 'Tiger? *Tiger?*'

They quickly searched all the corners of the hideout, but Tiger had gone. So, Cat pointed out, had Goldie's flame-thrower.

* * * * * *

Having slipped past the guards while their attention was on his friends, Tiger followed the same route he had taken that morning and, very quickly, found himself back at the department store. Rather than go inside, he crossed the road and cautiously approached the gates of the presidential palace. It didn't look as though there were even any guards posted. He could see some gardeners moving about in the shrubbery, but they showed no interest in him. He thought he caught a glimpse of a blonde head among them, but he couldn't be sure. Goldie wasn't the only girl with a blonde plait in the city – yet there was something familiar about the figure that made him think it was his friend.

'OK, Tiger, no one else is going to go in and save her. It's down to you,' he muttered, reaching out to give the gates a firm shove. He had a vague plan in mind: he would find her and conceal her somewhere in the department store until he and the others managed to find a cure.

The gates split apart and rolled back. *That was easy – far too easy*, he thought. Biting his lip, Tiger took a step forward. He could hear a high-pitched hum just on the edge of his perception. Sweat broke out on his brow and his skin stippled with goosebumps. Something was wrong. Surely there should be some kind of defence to get through? But it looked as though his way was clear to walk straight down the pathway and into the palace.

Then Tiger's eyes blurred. He rubbed them, trying

to clear his sight, his head aching. When he looked up he saw that the way was not undefended after all. Ten Krush warriors – the terrible robots under the command of Vilana – were stomping towards him. No, not ten: at least a hundred! Even the sky was thick with these horrible robots with their shiny armour and masked faces. They were going to capture him! He would be adapted, and he would never see his home again! He would become nothing more than a robotic servant of the Krush for all eternity!

Fumbling for the flame-thrower, Tiger screamed. The pain in his head increased to an unbearable level and he collapsed just as the first robot reached him.

Chapter 6 – The palace is defended

It hadn't taken Max, Cat and Ant long to guess where Tiger had gone.

'I'm going to kill him!' fumed Cat, as they ran down the stairs, forced to break their promise to Ida that they would stay put. They'd had to shrink to get past the guard – something they really hadn't wanted to risk. Now back at normal size, they were racing to catch up with Tiger. 'He shouldn't have run off like that. He didn't even give us a chance to go with him.'

Max tripped as he reached the landing of the fifteenth floor. 'I think that might've been my fault. Remember I mentioned rip-jumping out of here? He must have thought this was the best way to *make* us stay.'

'He should know us better than that,' muttered Cat.

They ran together towards the presidential palace. The light was waning as the suns set behind the mountains. Cat wasn't sorry to see the end of this awful day, but she would have preferred a few more hours of light for their search. It was bad enough contending with the Empty People during the day, but thinking of them lurking in the dark doorways was plain creepy.

They reached the gates and found them closed. There was no sign of Tiger.

'Do you think he's in there?' asked Ant.

Cat walked up to the bars and pointed. A flame-thrower was lying in the flower bed, half-hidden by the lush leaves. 'I'd say that's a *yes*.'

Max cleared his throat, summoning up his courage. 'OK team, let's do this together. We've been warned there is some kind of defence around this palace, but I can't see what it might be.' He visually checked for razor wire and electric fencing, but the gates seemed to be nothing but ordinary steel. 'Cat, you go for the flame-thrower. Ant and I will guard your back. Ready?'

They nodded.

'On the count of three then. One … two … three!' Max shoved the gates apart, surprised that they yielded so smoothly under his hands. Cat dived through the gap and grabbed the flame-thrower from the flower bed. All three waited for some kind of response to their invasion, but there was nothing, only a whistling sound almost too high to hear.

'Well, that was surprisingly easy,' said Cat. She turned to face her friends. 'Somehow I don't find that very reassuring … What now?'

But Max and Ant were staring in horror: Max was looking up at the darkening sky, Ant to the shadows on his left.

'Mordriss!' cried Max. 'Quick, take cover!'

'It's Vilana!' shouted Ant. 'She's coming for us!'

'What?' Cat couldn't see anyone coming and certainly not Mordriss – the Dimension Reaper – or his henchwoman, Vilana. 'Snap out of it, guys! You're imagining things.'

The whistling grew louder. Cat's eyes filled with unexpected tears. She had the sudden aching conviction that she would never see home again –

that she would be trapped forever rip-jumping between dimensions, that their mission would fail. Everything was futile. They should just give up now.

She looked to her friends. Max was punching the air, anger etched into lines on his face. Ant was trying to hide by climbing the nearest tree, beckoning to her to follow.

'I don't understand, guys,' Cat whispered. 'What are you doing? What can you see? Don't you know it's all hopeless in any case? We're never going home.' She slumped to her knees and let her tears fall on to the dusty road.

Chapter 7 – A new world

Tiger opened his eyes. Where was he? He seemed to be lying on the floor with his cheek pressed against cold tiles. The last thing he remembered was the Krush descending on him, but then he had blacked out. They hadn't assimilated him, had they? No, because he wouldn't even be asking that question if he had become one of their minions. He reached over his shoulder to feel the back of his neck. There was no Krush scorpion clamped there: proof he was still Tiger. *Phew!*

Once his worst fear had been dispelled, Tiger felt better able to face his present predicament. He heaved himself upright and rubbed his eyes. He was in a cell-like storage room. Flowerpots, gardening equipment and sacks of compost surrounded him. *The presidential palace. The Empty People gardeners.* Putting the hazy fragments together, he realized he must have passed out and been imprisoned here. So had he really seen the Krush or had that been his imagination playing tricks?

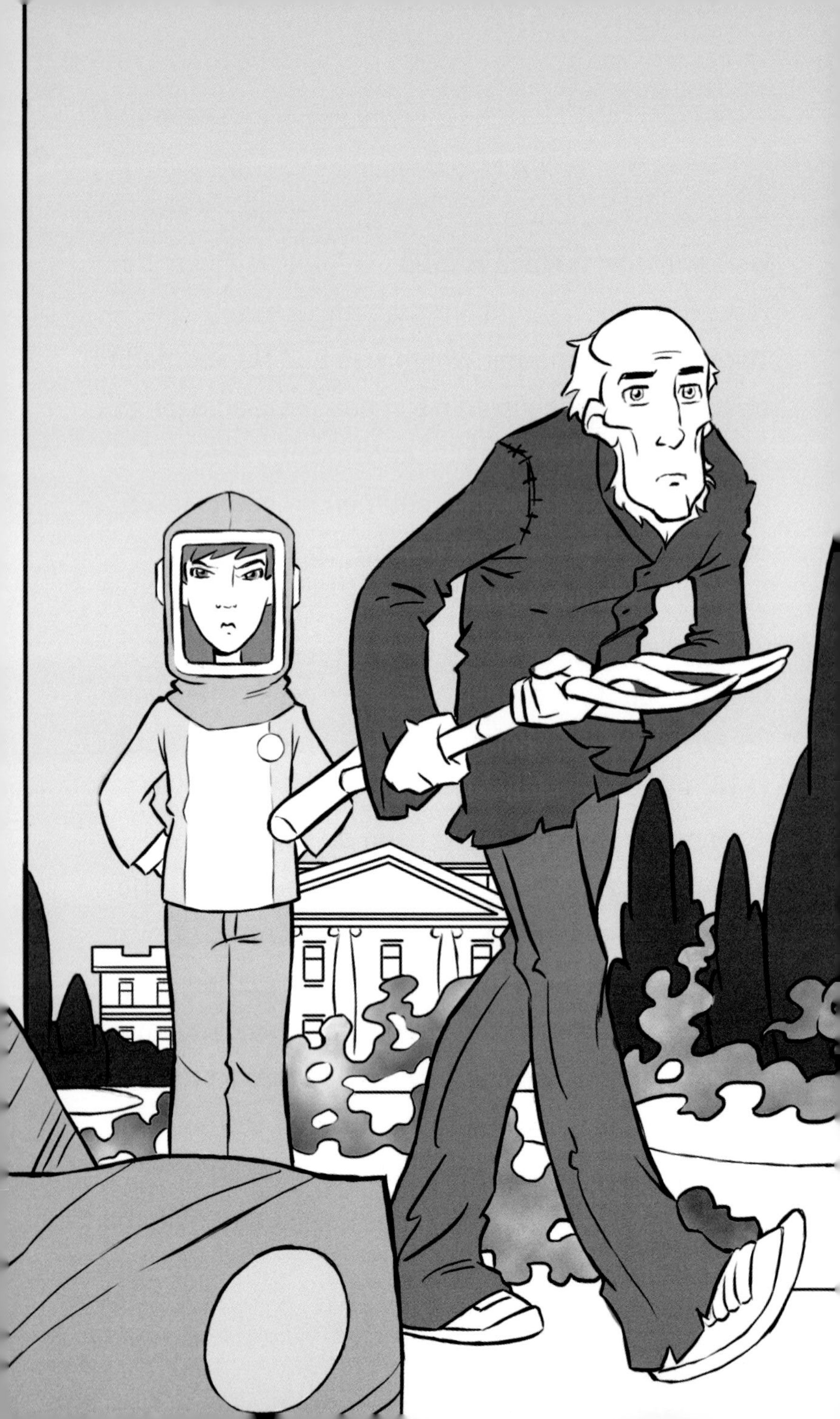

The door opened and an Empty Person shuffled in, pronged end of a garden fork pointing at Tiger. He was followed by a boy not much older than Tiger, who was dressed in a sky-blue suit and helmet. The helmet's clear visor meant that his features were visible – his dark, almost black, eyes and pale face.

'Another one?' sighed the boy, as if this really was too much to be bothered about. He pulled out a spray can from his pocket and squirted it directly in Tiger's face, releasing a puff of purple vapour.

Tiger sneezed. 'Why did you do that?' He coughed, eyes watering. Then he recognized the smell. 'It's you! You're the one releasing the mist!'

The boy frowned and shook the can. 'Why aren't you turning into one of them? That's not possible.'

Tiger stood up and tried to grab the can, but the boy shoved him back.

'Who are you?' demanded Tiger.

'You don't look right,' the boy continued, before turning to the guard. 'Mr President, take our visitor to the laboratory for tests. He isn't reacting like everyone else: I need to understand why.'

'Mr President!' exclaimed Tiger.

'Oh, don't you like what I've done to our former leader?' smirked the boy.

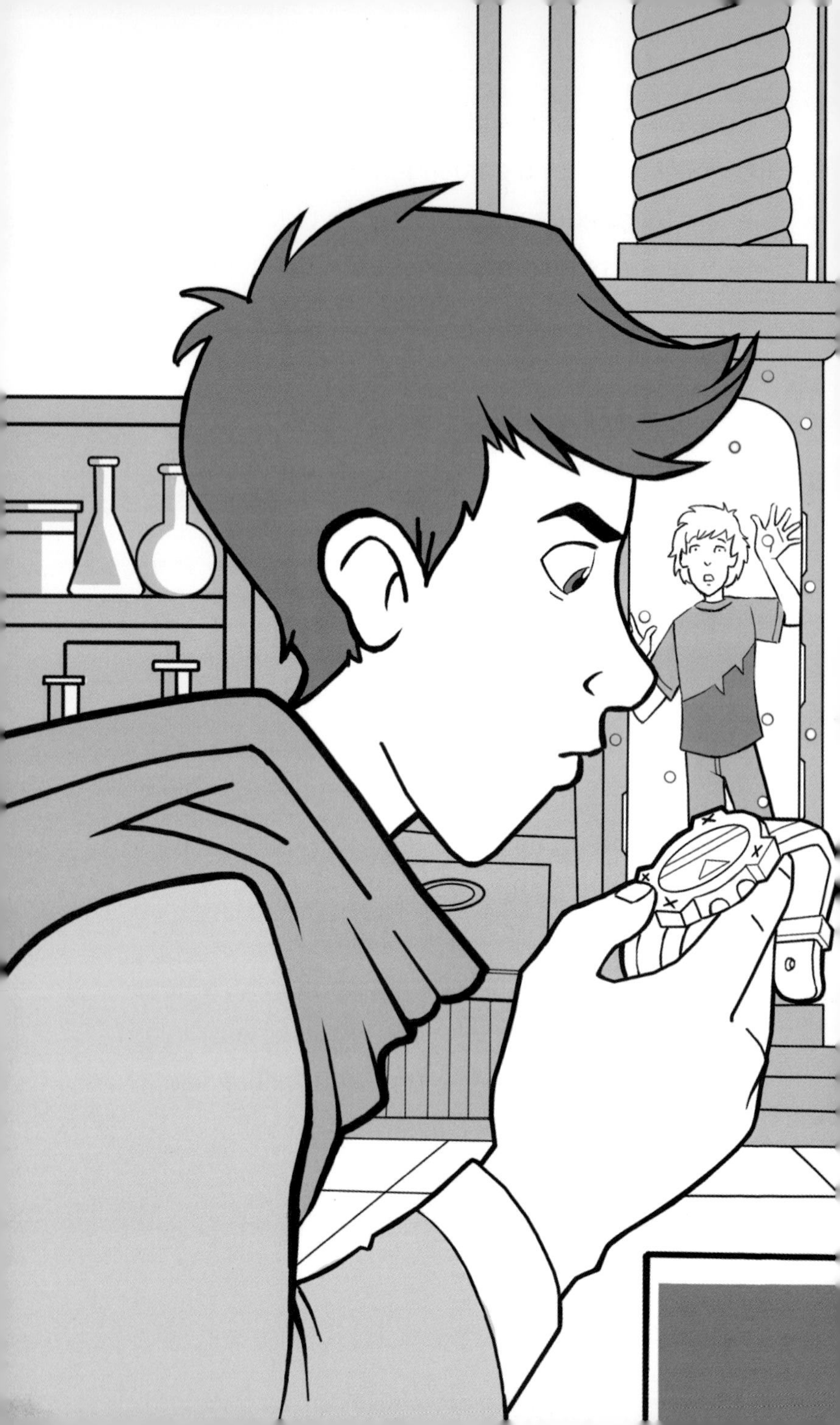

Five minutes later, after a fruitless struggle to escape the grip of the Empty President, Tiger found himself locked in a glass tube with holes punched in the sides, in a laboratory. He looked round. There were no windows, and they had descended lots of steps to get there, so he surmised he must be in the basement of the palace. In front of him, the boy danced around a complicated set of instruments, adjusting dials, making notes and ignoring the fact he had a live subject shouting protests at him from what resembled an enormous test tube. He cranked up the volume on his choice of music. The band sounded like heavy metal from Tiger's dimension but far less tuneful. Looking through the belongings that had been taken from his prisoner – a biscuit and a few loose coins – the boy became distracted by Tiger's watch. He held it under a bright lamp and pulled out a screwdriver.

Flooded with panic, Tiger thumped on the glass. 'Stop touching that! You don't understand what it can do!'

The boy looked up thoughtfully and waved a controller at the music centre to reduce the sound level. 'And you do?'

'Of course I do, it's mine.'

'Will you tell me?'

'Let me out of here and we'll see.'

The boy chuckled and shook his head. 'No deal.' He picked up the screwdriver again. 'There isn't an instrument that I don't know how to take apart and put back together again.'

'But it isn't from your dimension!' Tiger shouted in desperation. He'd never get away if the boy left his device in pieces on the desk.

The boy set the watch down and turned to his captive. 'Are you telling me the truth? Oh-ho, this is brilliant! Yes, I think you might be: you don't look like someone from Trist, not exactly. I thought maybe you were stunted in growth, but I think perhaps you might be another species.' He snapped his fingers. 'That would explain why the mist didn't work on you. Interesting. Hmm, I'll need to adjust the formula. Let's take a blood sample.' He approached the tube.

Tiger folded his arms. 'Let's not. Now you know I'm not from here, at least tell me what's going on. It won't matter to you, will it? I'm a stranger here – I can't do anything with the information.'

The boy licked his lips, tempted to share. *Of course*, thought Tiger, *he lives surrounded by brainless servants – he's probably desperate for someone to listen to his story.*

'All right, I'll tell you a little. My name is Tegan. I'm the best scientist in Trist.'

Tiger unfolded his arms, signalling he was listening. He was secretly thinking that Tegan was only the best scientist because he had turned all the others into Empty People. That was one way of getting rid of your rivals. 'Go on,' Tiger insisted.

'The scientists here didn't understand just how brilliant I was.' Tegan frowned at the memory. 'See him over there?' He pointed to a dusty-looking Empty Person filling up bottles of chemicals with a pipette. 'He used to teach me. Told me that I had to finish school before I joined the Guild of Scientists.'

'So you took your revenge, just because your teacher kept you back?'

'Oh no, not just that. What do you think I am? Stupid? No, I knew I would rise to the top very quickly, with or without a teacher like him.' Tegan leant against the edge of his workbench, getting into his stride. 'Everything changed on the first suns-rise of the New Year. My parents had been to a party and came home feeling unwell. They went to bed and never got up again. It turned out that they had caught marsh fever from another guest who had spread the disease through all our family and friends.' He brushed a speck of dust off his cuff, not meeting Tiger's eye.

'I'm sorry,' said Tiger.

Tegan cleared his throat. 'So was I. It was awful. I decided then and there that since I'd been given a much better brain than everyone else, surely I could prevent anyone – including myself – from feeling that way again? Far better to live safely and contentedly in my new world.' He gestured to his chemistry teacher. 'Like him.'

'How did you do it?'

'It was surprisingly simple. As the top science student in my year, I was invited to a reception at the palace to demonstrate my favourite experiment to the president. Everyone got rather more than they expected when I released my mist into the room. Once their minds were wiped, they were ready to receive my orders like a new piece of software slotted into a computer.'

The boy was power-crazed, Tiger decided. He wondered just how much of each person had been deleted. 'You're taking away their emotions?'

'Exactly.' Tegan stood up again. 'Or *suppressing* them might be a more accurate term. And I'll help you, too, so you won't be bothered by independent thoughts and feelings. I'm sure it won't take long to work out what element needs to be adjusted for your physiology. While I do that, you tell me about your world. I bet you never have to feel terrible emotions like those we are subjected to here?'

DIMENSION 0672
THE EMPTY PEOPLE

Trist was once a thriving capital city. It had been specially designed to be a pleasant city in which to live; it was full of open green spaces, light, airy buildings and environmentally-friendly transport.

All that changed when the mist arrived and three-quarters of the city's 2.5 million inhabitants suddenly began to transform. They seemed to lose their personalities and began to wander the city, seemingly aimlessly. Almost immediately, the animals of the city fled and the plants began to die.

Survivors have long been trying to work on a cure. So far they have tried:

– counter mists, made from blending water and different natural oils,

– oxygen therapy,

– musical communication.

The best scientists are researching a vaccination against the mist but, so far, trials have not been successful.

There was so much wrong about what Tegan had said that Tiger didn't know where to start. 'Look, Tegan, I don't want to have my emotions taken from me.'

Tegan shook his head and smiled in an 'I-know-better' way.

'You've not wiped your own mind,' Tiger continued. 'So you must realize it is better to live and feel things – the bad stuff as well as the good?'

'I can't do it to myself or I wouldn't be able to help everyone else,' Tegan replied, rooting through a case for the instruments he needed to take a blood sample.

'But you're not giving them a choice!'

'No. I tried that and they wouldn't obey me. Ah-ha! Here it is.' Tegan approached the capsule and fitted the instrument in a mechanical arm that he could direct towards Tiger like one of those picker machines with a claw. 'Now, just hold still. This won't hurt.'

Chapter 8 – Worst fears

This was all wrong. Kneeling between the gates to the palace, Cat battled her feeling of hopelessness. It wasn't like her to capitulate like this, not when her friends were in danger. She was the sort who would carry on fighting, even when all chance of success was gone.

Raising her head, Cat searched for Max and Ant. Up in his tree, Ant was swiping at the air, defending himself against an invisible Vilana. Max was throwing rocks and dodging behind the hedges in a pitched battle against …

Against nothing.

Both her friends were fighting different illusions. She had been brought to her knees by the belief she would never see her home again – her own secret fear.

Cat realized then what was happening. The palace was defended not by gates and walls, but by a high-pitched sound that triggered their deepest anxieties: Max saw Mordriss; Ant fought Vilana; she was made powerless by the idea that they were lost forever rip-jumping.

Cat stuck her fingers in her ears and immediately the feeling of hopelessness subsided. Where was the sound coming from? Humming loudly to counteract the noise, she dropped her hand to grab the flame-thrower. Then she spotted speakers placed along the fence – four of them. Ignoring her friends' frantic shouts to take cover and hide from Vilana and Mordriss, she pointed the hose at the first of the speakers, pressed the canister button and burnt the speaker to a crisp. The intensity of the noise abated slightly. The second speaker went the same way. By the third, Ant was shaking his head, patting his ears.

When the fourth was silenced, Max stood, fists clenched, looking about him in confusion. 'What happened to Mordriss?'

Ant crawled down from his tree. 'Was it the noise?'

Cat nodded. 'Yes. It was tuned to trigger a vivid illusion of your deepest fear.'

Ant clapped her on the back. 'Well done for working that out! I guess that means you're not scared of anything? I'm impressed.'

Cat shivered. 'Oh, I have my fear, but it's not something physical you can fight. I don't think the person behind this defensive strategy anticipated that.'

Max was still shaking from his life-and-death battle with a shadow. 'I can't believe that wasn't real.'

'I know. I feel the same way. Would you just check, Cat, that Vilana really isn't here?' asked Ant sheepishly. 'I mean, I can see that she isn't, but I just can't shake the feeling that she is.'

Cat checked her watch. 'No, there's no sign of her.'

Max coughed loudly. 'Time to go. The Empty People are approaching. I think they are expecting us to be subdued by our fight for survival.'

Ant fell flat on the ground. 'Quick, copy me!'

With a groan, Cat lay down, too.

'You have a plan?' Max asked as he sprawled on the grass verge. 'Why aren't we running?'

'Because this must be what happened to Tiger,' hissed Ant. 'We know these people don't feel the emotion to be cruel. They'll pick us up and take us to the palace … and to Tiger. It's the quickest way.'

'I hope you know what you're doing,' Max muttered.

'No, but have you got a better idea?'

Just as Ant predicted, three Empty People arrived and threw the newcomers over their shoulders. Carried like sacks, the friends were taken into the palace and down a cold flight of steps. Cat could hear voices, but all she could see were white marble stairs.

'Now, just hold still. This won't hurt,' a voice was saying.

'Get away from me!' a familiar voice yelled. It was Tiger, and he sounded like he was in trouble.

The lead Empty Person kicked open a door and grunted.

'What! Not more of them?' said the first voice. Cat twisted her head and saw a boy in a sky-blue suit standing in front of a glass capsule containing Tiger.

'Now!' roared Max. The three friends twisted round and escaped from their captors, dropping to the ground.

'Remember, they're scared of fire!' shouted Ant, grabbing a blowtorch off the workbench and giving it a warning squeeze.

'Get out of here!' squawked the boy. 'No one is allowed in here without my permission.' He lunged towards Ant and knocked over a bottle of chemicals. As Ant gave another squeeze of the blowtorch, a ripple of flame caught on the liquid the boy had spilled. It ran over the desk and dropped to the floor, weaving in a line of flame between the friends and the Empty People. Cat ran to the capsule and thumped the door release. Tiger tumbled out. Cat turned and headed for the stairs.

'No, no! You can't leave!' the boy yelled, as he tried to block Tiger's escape.

'Oh yes we can, Tegan!' said Tiger. He pushed past him and rushed to the workbench. 'Where's my watch? It's gone!'

The flames were taking hold. Thick smoke coiled in the air, a poisonous green. The Empty People were already lurching towards the stairs.

'Evacuate!' shouted Ant.

Cat grabbed Tiger who was searching frantically under the workbench. 'We've got to leave.'

'My watch!'

'There's no time!'

Potions and chemicals started to explode as the fire took hold of the laboratory supplies. Max and Ant seized Tegan and dragged him up the stairs. The flames followed, eating up the plush blue carpet and gold-fringed drapes of the great entrance hall. Joined by hundreds of fleeing Empty People, they ran through the palace and out on to the lawn in front of the main ceremonial chamber.

'My palace!' wailed Tegan. 'My equipment.'

Cat had no sympathy to spare for him. She was worried about the Empty People who were cowering in terror by the garden fountain. Among the many figures she spotted a distinctive blonde head.

'Goldie!' She ran to their friend and pulled her from the crowd. 'Don't worry. The fire won't reach you here.'

Goldie spun in a petrified circle, hands flapping as if she were trying to fly away.

Tiger pushed Tegan towards the Empty People. 'I thought you said they didn't feel anything! Look at them: they're terrified!'

'I had to leave a few basic instincts intact,' moaned Tegan. 'If I hadn't, they wouldn't have known that they mustn't touch fire – they would have been hurt.'

'You control them: tell them they're safe!' ordered Tiger.

'They won't listen. Their fear is more powerful than any order I can give. That's why they run from flame-throwers even when I've told them the other people won't harm them.'

The flames broke out of the upper windows with a shattering of glass and a belch of smoke.

'We've got to get further away. Let's lead them to safety ourselves,' suggested Max.

'Lead them where?' Ant asked.

'It doesn't matter as long as it isn't on fire.' Max clapped his hands. 'Come on, people: follow me!'

It was no good – the Empty People didn't listen.

Cat rubbed her eyes, stinging from the smoke. 'Remember how Goldie followed the other Empty People? Why don't we see if we can get her to lead them away. Goldie? Goldie?' She took her friend's hand and tugged. 'Come on.'

Happy to be taken further from the flames, Goldie stumbled after Cat. It was like one sheep leading others out of a field: all the Empty People obediently turned and followed Goldie.

Tiger gripped Tegan's elbow, making sure he didn't escape. 'And you think this is a better life for them?'

Tegan bit his lip and looked down.

'What do we do with him?' asked Max.

'I vote we take him to the elders; they can deal with him. Fortunately, he's their problem,' Tiger replied. 'I don't want to spend another second with him. He's the reason my watch is gone.'

It was only then that the others realized exactly how far their mission had gone awry.

'Oh, no,' groaned Cat. 'Whatever can we do now?' She realized her worst fear might be coming true after all. They'd never be able to leave if they were missing a watch.

Chapter 9 – **Shrinking feeling**

They made an odd procession as they walked to the central square, the only place the friends could think of that was big enough to keep all the Empty People together. More and more joined the evacuees from the palace, stumbling out of doorways and underground stations.

Tiger thrust his hands into his pockets and kicked at the dust. He'd done it. He'd ruined the mission. How could he have let his watch go? He hated how his friends exchanged worried looks behind his back, keen not to blame him, but silently knowing their mission was over.

'Look, it's OK, guys. We'll come up with a plan,' he said quietly. 'Let's get Tegan to the elders and worry about us later.' Despite his attempts at a brave face, Tiger was still angry with himself. If he hadn't been so impulsive, he would never have plunged them all into this new crisis. He had wanted to be a hero but had ended up needing to be rescued himself. Worse still, they were little closer to saving Goldie.

'Tell us about this boy,' said Max, swiftly changing the subject.

Tiger quickly filled them in on Tegan's story. He grimaced when he admitted that he had told the other boy that they were from another dimension – another moment of which he was not proud. 'Apparently he did all this out of some warped desire to make people happier,' he concluded.

'Not happier,' corrected Tegan. 'Just not sad. See, these people aren't suffering. They're quite content to amble about the city with me telling them what to do.'

'That's the most idiotic thing I've ever heard!' exclaimed Cat. 'I can't believe you really think that! Who made you judge and jury over everyone else in your dimension?'

'I'm the cleverest person I know, so I am best placed to decide.'

'You know, I looked up the definition of arrogant in the dictionary and found a picture of him,' Ant murmured to Tiger.

They finally arrived at the central square. It quickly began filling up with the procession of Empty People.

'Do you think these people will obey you now?' Max asked Tegan.

'Yes. I've trained them to follow my orders.'

Tiger looked at Tegan. He knew enough about him to guess he was planning to turn the Empty People against the friends. 'Stop right there!' said Tiger, poking Tegan in the ribs. 'Don't even *consider* saying any of what you are thinking.'

'How do *you* know what I'm thinking?' sneered Tegan.

'You may think you're clever, but actually you're really predictable.' Tiger pointed to the statue of the fallen horsewoman. 'Stand there and tell these people to sit down and not panic.'

After a moment's consideration, Tegan pointed to the ground. Like one vast, well-trained army, every single Empty Person sat.

Tegan gave a smug smile. 'Happy now? I've done what you suggested, so why don't you let me go?'

'No way. You need to face your own people – the ones you've not poisoned,' Max said firmly.

Tegan reached into his pocket and extracted Tiger's watch. 'How about I swap this for my freedom?'

'My watch!' Tiger made a swipe for it, but before he could reach it, Tegan had dodged behind the closest of his Empty People.

'Give that back!' shouted Cat.

Tegan jumped up on to the statue's plinth. 'No! Not unless you free me.'

'Never. You have to be brought to justice,' Ant told him. 'You're too dangerous to let loose.'

'Well, would it change your mind if I admitted that not everything was my idea? That 'fear fence' of mine, that you all got caught up in? That was suggested to me by a most interesting visitor. Is she from your dimension?'

'Who was that?' asked Cat, although she could take a good guess.

'She said her name was Vilana, and she was most impressed by the changes I had made to Trist.'

'Vilana!' exclaimed Ant. 'Yes, I can see her loving all this.'

'Well done,' said Cat sarcastically. 'You've managed to impress one of the cruellest people in all the known dimensions.'

'Cruel?' Tegan frowned. 'She seemed quite pleasant to me.'

'If you think releasing mass destruction on all living things is pleasant … Where is she now?' Cat pressed.

'She had to leave,' Tegan said smugly. 'Under pressure to do something, she said. She promised to come back and see how I was getting on.'

'If she comes back, trust me, you won't want to be here.' Ant turned to Tiger. 'He really is gullible, isn't he?'

'I think he's just very, very sad,' said Tiger, treating Tegan to a contemptuous look.

Pity was the last thing that Tegan wanted. 'I am not gullible or sad!' He brandished Tiger's watch and strapped it on his own wrist. 'I'll figure this out myself and then you'll be sorry.'

Tiger cowered. 'Whatever you do, don't turn the dial and press the X!'

'But …!' protested Cat.

Tiger hushed her with a look.

'Hah! Big mistake!' With great glee, Tegan stabbed

at the dial. Immediately, he started to shrink. 'What ... what's happening?'

Ready for this to happen, Tiger dived for Tegan and trapped him under his hands. Picking up the struggling, micro-sized boy by the waist, he slipped the micro-watch off Tegan's wrist.

'Actually, Ant, you were right about the gullible bit,' Tiger grinned.

Chapter 10 – **Full people**

The huge gathering of Empty People attracted the survivors from the skyscrapers. The four friends could see them approaching the square with their flame-throwers.

'Hey! Don't use them!' shouted Max. The last thing they wanted was to cause a stampede. Max rushed up to the survivors, desperate to convince them that the Empty People weren't a threat.

After a brief consultation, Ida, Joel and Merrie approached warily. The Empty People remained motionless. They had been instructed to sit down by Tegan and would not move again until he gave them another order. He was unable to do so – Tiger had put him inside a little temporary prison made up of bricks and stones from the broken buildings. His voice could be heard squeaking inside, but not loudly enough to reach even the nearest of his Empty People.

'Let me out! I'll get you for this!' Tegan yelled.

'No, you won't,' said Tiger firmly, through the roof of cracked slate. 'You'll sit and have a think about what it feels like to be in someone else's power.'

The noise from inside subsided.

'What's going on here?' asked Ida.

'Ah,' said Max. 'That's rather a long story.' They each took turns recounting their part in the day's events: Tiger's capture, Cat's brainwave about the fence, the disaster in the palace, and the unveiling of the boy behind the whole sorry chain of events that had brought Trist to this terrible state.

'He's in there, is he?' growled Merrie.

'Yes,' said Tiger.

'I don't believe you,' murmured Ida.

'Then take a look.' Tiger lifted the lid to reveal the grumpy micro-scientist sitting in a corner.

'Why is he so small?'

'It was an experiment,' began Cat.

'That went wrong,' finished Tiger.

'Can you put him back to the right size?' Ida asked.

'Do you want him back? I mean, I think he is less likely to cause trouble as he is,' Tiger pointed out.

Ida tapped her fingers against the stone plinth, thinking. 'I propose a bargain: we restore him if he cures all the Empty People.'

'Fair enough. Tegan, did you hear that?'

'Yes,' said Tegan curtly.

'Can you do it?'

'I might be able to.' He folded his arms and stuck his nose in the air.

Tiger showed him the watch. 'Think carefully. Can you do it or do you want to stay in a micro-prison for the rest of your life?'

'Yes, all right. I can do it.'

Tiger turned to Ida. 'I don't trust him.'

'Nor do I. That is why he is going to give Joel here the formula *before* he is restored to normal size. Joel?'

Goldie's uncle stepped closer. 'I used to be a chemistry teacher before all the schools were closed down,' he explained.

'He isn't that keen on chemistry teachers,' warned Tiger.

'That's fine, I'm not very keen on him. So, Tegan, tell me what I need to know.'

Half an hour later, after a long discussion and many notes, Joel signalled he had what he needed. 'Keep everyone here. I'll be back in a couple of hours.'

People from the hideouts brought them food and drink to pass the time. Some found their loved ones among the Empty People. Cat was delighted to see them sitting next to children or parents, stroking their hair, tying shoelaces or tidying up their clothing. Now there was hope of a cure, they were no longer scared of their close proximity.

Joel returned, hauling a huge vat of liquid on a cart. 'Here it is. This should work.'

'How do we deliver the dosage to them?' asked Ida.

'Convert the flame-throwers. They can be used to pump this liquid instead.'

Joel gently doused Goldie in a fine mist of the new, green liquid and she closed her eyes and slumped to the ground. The friends watched as the survivors filled up their canisters and spread out through the square spraying the Empty People. It was like watching hypnotists send a whole crowd to sleep. One by one, the Empty People closed their eyes and folded forward.

'You *are* curing them, aren't you?' asked Ant, anxiously.

'I hope so,' said Joel, glancing at the little prison. 'I did exactly as Tegan said.'

'You'd better not have double-crossed us,' warned Tiger through the roof.

'Didn't!' shouted Tegan, still in a foul mood.

'Tiger!' called Cat. 'Look at Goldie!'

Goldie's eyes were fluttering open. 'What …?'

'Goldie! Do you remember us?' asked Cat.

'Yes, of course. But how did we get here? I remember the mist … and a fire … and a long walk – but only vaguely. It feels like a dream.'

'You became an Empty Person, but your Uncle Joel has cooked up an antidote,' Cat explained gently.

Goldie's eyes filled with tears of joy. 'He did? Oh, and will everyone be all right? My parents? My sister?'

'Yes, everyone,' Cat said, smiling.

Goldie got to her feet and looked down at her stained clothes. 'Oh dear – I need a shower!'

Ida stepped forward and hugged her. 'Everybody needs a shower, Goldie. It's been quite a day. But, thanks to your friends, it has all ended very well indeed. Where did you say you were from?' she asked the friends.

'We didn't,' said Max, then hastily shifted the subject. 'Let's get Tegan back to his proper size so Tiger can have his watch returned to him permanently. Tiger?'

'OK. Max, Cat: this will work best if you shrink and keep hold of him as you grow back to normal size. I wouldn't put it past him to run.' Tiger extricated Tegan from his prison. 'Ready?'

'Yes,' said Cat. She shrank to Tegan's height and grabbed his arm firmly. 'Watch your step, Tegan.'

'Ready when you are,' confirmed Max, joining her and taking the other arm.

'Together now: hit your dials.'

Goldie and Ida watched in amazement as three full-sized figures appeared side by side.

'Are you sure this isn't a dream?' Goldie asked.

'Quite sure,' Ant replied, with a small smile.

Max and Cat marched Tegan over to Ida.

'He's all yours,' said Max. 'Thank goodness.'

Ida signalled to Merrie and another man to take Tegan away. 'Lock the boy up, please. The council will meet to decide his punishment as soon as we have made sure every single Empty Person is back to normal once more.'

Grouching and complaining, Tegan was led away.

'I'm glad to see the back of him,' admitted Tiger. 'He really is dangerous. He has scientific sense but no common sense.'

'Don't worry. We will make sure he never sees inside a laboratory again. As long as no one has been irreparably harmed by his mist, I think he might find he has a long future ahead of him as a gardener. He can turn his attention to plants and flowers instead,' said Ida.

'I'd say that is the perfect punishment. He can try brewing rebellion among the carrots and see how far he gets!' Tiger laughed.

Goldie came over with two adults and a little girl who looked rather like her. 'Max, Cat, Ant, Tiger: I'd like you to meet my parents and my little sister.' She beamed at them. 'Mum, Dad: these are the amazing new friends I told you about.'

Goldie's father cleared his throat. 'This is all very confusing, but I understand we have you to thank for our return to normal?'

The friends felt their cheeks redden. 'Well, Joel made the antidote,' Ant said quickly.

'And we wouldn't have survived the first day without Goldie,' added Cat.

'I hope you will feel very welcome to stay with us – that is, if we still have a house to go to?' said Goldie's mother, gazing around the square, bewildered at how fast it had gone to rack and ruin. 'Oh my! It appears we've a lot of work ahead to put things right.'

The friends exchanged a look. They also had a mission that they could not neglect.

'Shall we?' prompted Max.

'I'm afraid we must,' said Cat.

Tiger smiled regretfully at Goldie. 'I'm so pleased you've got your family back.'

'What? Where are you going?' asked Goldie.

'You go and catch up with your family,' said Cat.

'Yeah, don't worry about us,' added Ant. 'Thanks for everything.'

'I'm picking up a fresh signal!' Cat exclaimed, tapping Max's arm in excitement.

Ant set his watch to the dimension number Cat read out. 'By the way, two suns,' he said to Goldie. 'That is so great. You have a beautiful world.'

On Max's signal, they twisted their dials three times anticlockwise and vanished.

Goldie gaped. 'Where have they gone?'

'They were from another dimension!' wailed Tegan from over by the edge of the square. 'You let them go, and now it's too late to study them!'

Goldie laughed and hugged her little sister. 'Then I'm glad they managed to get away. Now,' she continued, taking her sister's hand, 'I think I should tell you all about the four wonderful friends who saved us.' Together they started to walk back home.

NEXT ... The Beasts of Blackwater